ROTHERHAM PUBLIC LIBRARIES

VIKING/PUFFIN

Published by the Penguin Group
Penguin Books Ltd, 27 Wrights Lane, London W8 5TZ, England
Penguin Books USA Inc., 375 Hudson Street, New York, New York 10014, USA
Penguin Books Australia Ltd, Ringwood, Victoria, Australia
Penguin Books Canada Ltd, 10 Alcorn Avenue, Toronto, Ontario, Canada M4V 3B2
Penguin Books (NZ) Ltd, 182–190 Wairau Road, Auckland 10, New Zealand

Penguin Books Ltd, Registered Offices: Harmondsworth, Middlesex, England

First published 1997
1 3 5 7 9 10 8 6 4 2

Text copyright © Penguin Books Ltd, 1997
Illustrations copyright © Steve Cox, 1997

The moral right of the illustrator has been asserted

Manufactured in China by Imago

British Library Cataloguing in Publication Data
A CIP catalogue record for this book is available from the British Library

ISBN 0–670–87258–X Hardback
ISBN 0–140–56208–7 Paperback

BIG MACHINES
IN TOWN
STEVE COX

Puffin

Viking

BUILDING A PLAYGROUND

EXCAVATOR

9

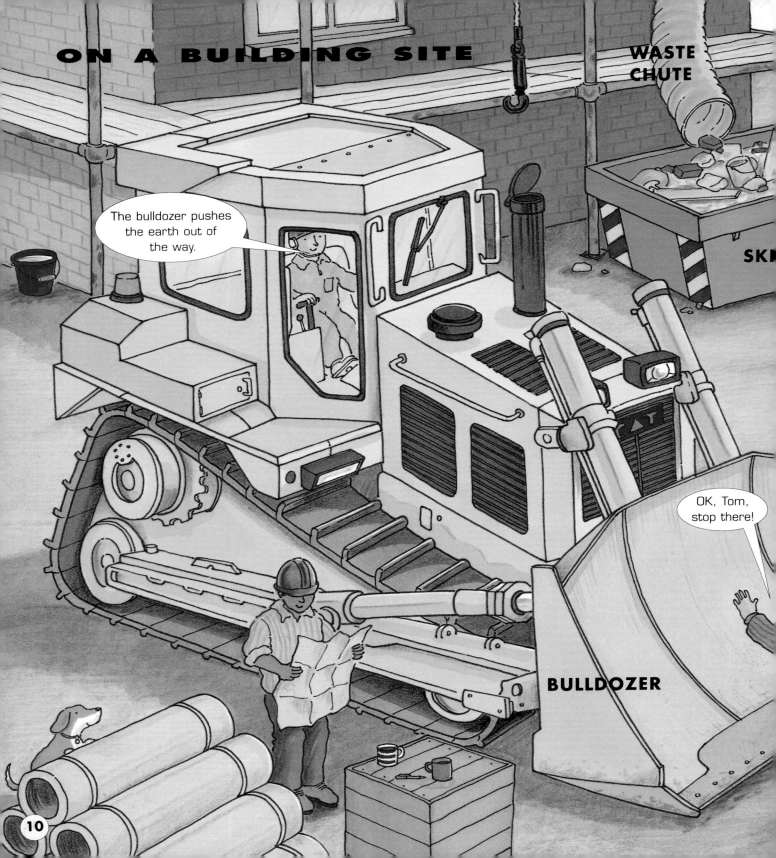

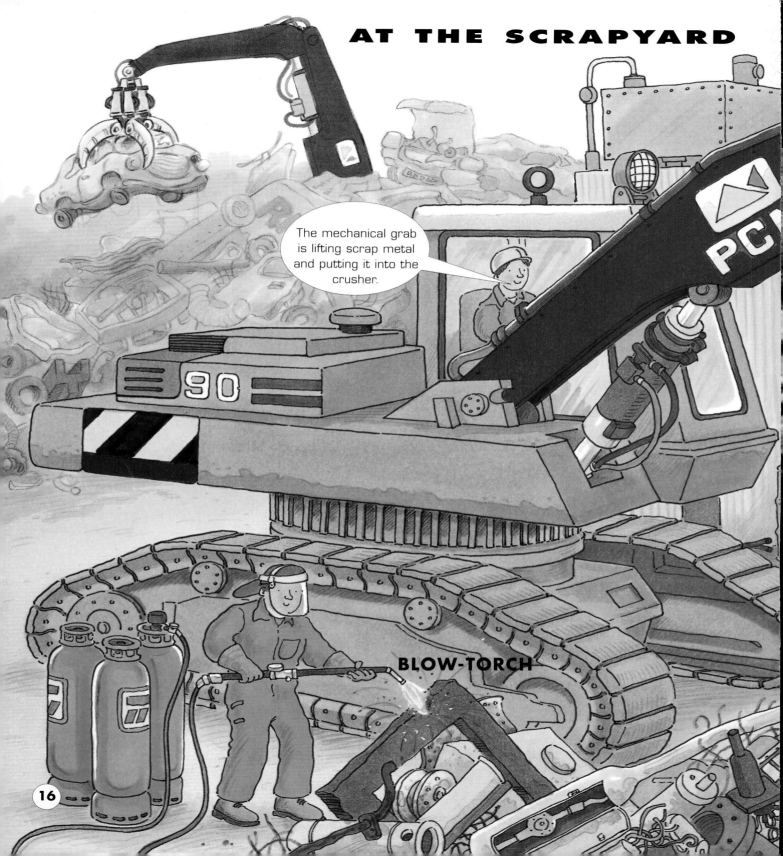

BIG MACHINES IN TOWN

Follow Ben and his dad through the pages of this book:

Ben and his dad are shopping in town.

"Look, Dad! A fire engine!" says Ben.

The fire engine has a hydraulic lift platform, which lifts the firefighters up high. They shoot water at the fire from the water cannon.

"What happens if the water runs out?" asks Ben.

"The firefighters can get more water from the fire hydrant," Dad tells him. "It's like a big tap under the pavement."

Ben's friend, Jim, is in town with his family.

They are watching some workers building a new playground. One of them drives the excavator which digs up the earth. Another uses a drill to make holes in the rocky ground. The cement mixer turns round and round mixing sand, cement and gravel together to make concrete.

Near by, the workers are building houses.

Tom's bulldozer is used to push earth out of the way. The back of the dump truck lifts up so that the stones empty on to the ground.

The houses need a new road. The men are working hard. The scraper clears away the earth. Then the paver lays the tarmac on the new road. The roller makes the tarmac smooth and flat.

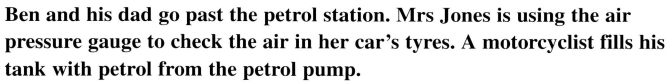

Ben and his dad go past the petrol station. Mrs Jones is using the air pressure gauge to check the air in her car's tyres. A motorcyclist fills his tank with petrol from the petrol pump.

"What is Mr Smith doing?" asks Ben.

"He's in the automatic car wash," says Dad. "The machine is cleaning his car for him while he has a rest."

Ben and his dad walk home past the scrapyard.

They watch as the mechanical grab lifts up an old car.

"It will go into the crusher next," Dad tells Ben. "The crusher squashes the metal up."

"Poor old car," says Ben.

INDEX

AIR PRESSURE GAUGE	14	HYDRAULIC LIFT PLATFORM	7
BLOW-TORCH	16	MECHANICAL GRAB	17
BULLDOZER	10	PAVER	13
CAR WASH	14	PETROL PUMP	15
CEMENT MIXER	9,11	POLICE CAR	6
COMPRESSOR	9	ROLLER	12
CRUSHER	17	SCRAPER	13
DRILL	9	SKIP	11
DUMP TRUCK	11	TARMAC	13
EXCAVATOR	8	TYRES	14
FIRE ENGINE	6	VACUUM CLEANER	15
FIRE EXTINGUISHER	14	WASTE CHUTE	10
GRAB	17	WATER CANNON	7
HOSE	7	WATER HYDRANT	7